CUTTING-EDGE TECHNOLOGY

ALL ABOUT ARTIFICIAL INTELLIGENCE

by Joanne Mattern

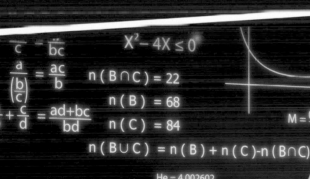

FOCUS READERS®

NAVIGATOR

WWW.FOCUSREADERS.COM

Focus Readers is distributed by North Star Editions:
sales@northstareditions.com | 888-417-0195

Produced for Focus Readers by Red Line Editorial.

Content Consultant: Jim Davis, PhD, Professor of Computer Science and Engineering, Ohio State University

Photographs ©: Shutterstock Images, cover, 1, 7, 8–9, 12, 16, 18, 21, 25; iStockphoto, 4–5, 11, 14–15, 22–23, 26–27, 28

Library of Congress Cataloging-in-Publication Data
Names: Mattern, Joanne, 1963- author.
Title: All about artificial intelligence / by Joanne Mattern.
Description: Lake Elmo, MN : Focus Readers, [2023] | Series: Cutting-edge technology | Includes bibliographical references and index. | Audience: Grades 4-6
Identifiers: LCCN 2022031702 (print) | LCCN 2022031703 (ebook) | ISBN 9781637394700 (hardcover) | ISBN 9781637395073 (paperback) | ISBN 9781637395776 (ebook pdf) | ISBN 9781637395448 (hosted ebook)
Subjects: LCSH: Artificial intelligence--Juvenile literature.
Classification: LCC Q335.4 .M38 2023 (print) | LCC Q335.4 (ebook) | DDC 006.3--dc23/eng20220919
LC record available at https://lccn.loc.gov/2022031702
LC ebook record available at https://lccn.loc.gov/2022031703

Printed in the United States of America
Mankato, MN
012023

ABOUT THE AUTHOR

Joanne Mattern has written hundreds of books for young readers. Her favorite topics are science, history, and sports. She loves researching, writing, and learning new things! Mattern lives in New York State with her family and enjoys reading, doing jigsaw puzzles, and hiking.

CHAPTER 2

HOW AI WORKS

Computers perform tasks by following sets of instructions. These instructions are called code. Humans write the code. To do so, they break each task into a series of steps for a computer to follow.

Usually, computers need instructions for each step of a process. But AI can

People who write code are called programmers.

allow computers to make decisions and solve problems on their own. Algorithms are the key to how AI works. An algorithm is a set of instructions for a particular task. Algorithms tell computers what to do at each step. But the algorithms used in AI can be more complex. They can allow computers to learn and make decisions. These algorithms look for patterns. The patterns shape how the computers respond.

For example, some algorithms choose what ads people see on websites. The algorithms track the websites each person visits. Based on this **data**, the algorithms guess what the person might

Websites often use AI to show products that other users also bought or searched for.

want to buy. Suppose a person searches for boots. Then the person looks at websites for shoe stores. The algorithm might start showing more ads for shoes.

To learn tasks, algorithms use huge amounts of data. Suppose a computer

AI can learn to recognize and translate words.

needed to label photos of cats and dogs.
First, it would look at thousands of
labeled pictures. It would study what both
cats and dogs looked like. It would find
patterns to tell them apart.

Then, the computer would be tested.
It would look at new photos. It would
try to label the animal in each photo.
Similar processes help computers learn to

recognize faces, words, and much more. In fact, some AI can write text or change words from one language to another.

AI can also give instructions to other machines. For example, AI can control robots. These machines can do jobs that would be hard or risky for people.

JEOPARDY! CHAMP

In 2011, a computer named Watson defeated two top players on the popular TV game show *Jeopardy!* Watson studied past questions from the show. It played 100 practice games against past winners. Watson also used **software** that studied language and information. As a result, Watson could process 200 million pages of data and answer questions correctly in just a few seconds.

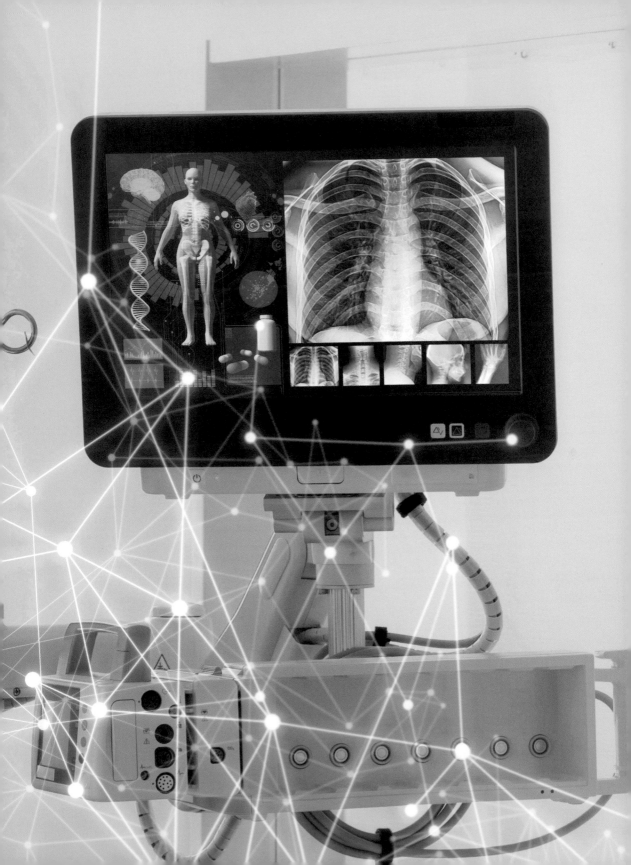

CHAPTER 3

USES OF ARTIFICIAL INTELLIGENCE

People and businesses use AI every day. For example, AI has been very helpful in health care. AI can look at medical scans. It can diagnose diseases faster and more accurately than doctors can. AI can also identify the best drugs to treat diseases. As a result, patients live longer.

AI can help doctors look for problems in X-rays and scans.

Map apps use AI to find several routes and calculate how long each one will take.

Apps such as Google Maps and Waze use AI to give drivers directions. These apps can find the fastest route. They can alert drivers to problems such as accidents or road construction. And they can find a new route if a driver makes a wrong turn.

AI can control self-driving cars as well. A computer steers the car and takes in information about its surroundings. It watches for road markings, traffic lights, and signs. AI uses these details to guide the car along its route. It also looks out for other people and vehicles.

The internet uses AI in many ways. Some websites have chatbots. These computer programs talk to people and answer questions. AI also helps with online shopping. It can help suggest products to users. For example, if a user searches for "brown winter jackets," AI

Chatbots can talk to customers while business owners are busy with other tasks.

can show clothes that fit this description. It may recommend similar items, too. Often, these include products that previous users bought or searched for at the same time.

AI can also help prevent **fraud**. To do so, it tracks a person's shopping habits.

If it sees a purchase that seems unusual, it alerts the person or the bank. For example, suppose a person lives in New York. If that person's credit card is used to buy jewelry in Ireland, AI can flag the purchase. It can make sure a thief isn't trying to use the card.

AI IN GAMING

In many video games, non-playable characters (NPCs) are controlled by the computer. AI helps them react to what a player does. It chooses what the NPCs do and say. AI can also change the challenges that players face throughout the game. It may respond to each player's skill. It can make the game harder as players improve.

VIRTUAL ASSISTANTS

Virtual assistants such as Apple's Siri or Amazon's Alexa use AI to respond to voice commands. They can answer questions or do simple tasks. This process takes several steps.

First, the device needs to hear and understand what the person is saying. It breaks down each word into smaller sounds. AI analyzes these sounds. It uses data and **context** to figure out what words the speaker is saying.

Next, AI determines what action or answer the user wants. It goes through a series of possible answers. It calculates which one will most likely be helpful.

Finally, the virtual assistant does the requested action. Virtual assistants often find information on the internet. Many can also control devices.

AI & VOICE COMMANDS

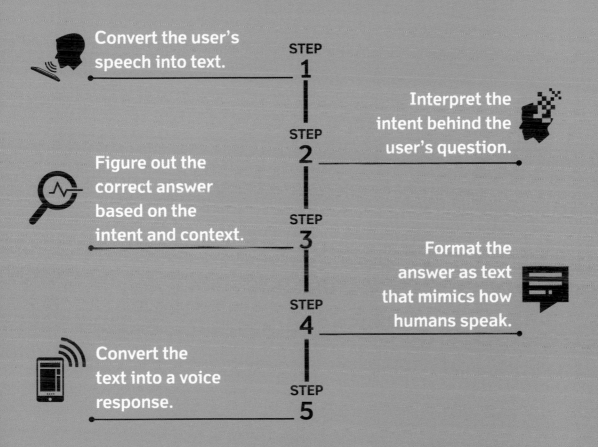

STEP 1 — Convert the user's speech into text.

STEP 2 — Interpret the intent behind the user's question.

STEP 3 — Figure out the correct answer based on the intent and context.

STEP 4 — Format the answer as text that mimics how humans speak.

STEP 5 — Convert the text into a voice response.

For example, Alexa can turn lights on or off. Siri can send messages or make phone calls. Virtual assistants may also control cars or appliances.

SHOP ONLINE

SALES

FREE Shipping & Special OFFER

| Fitness Clothes | Baby Care | Women's Shoes | Beauty Products |
| High | Office | Men's | Women's |

credit

CHAPTER 4

POTENTIAL DANGERS

Artificial intelligence has made people's lives easier in many ways. However, many people worry about how it affects their privacy. When people use AI, it often collects and stores data about them. This information can include their interests or even their locations. This data can be sold to companies. Data may also

When people use websites, their activity or payment information can be tracked or stolen.

be stolen. People's information can be shared without their knowledge.

People also worry about how AI makes decisions. AI relies on data that comes from humans. So, it can absorb and act on people's **biases**. In addition, AI is designed to achieve a goal. So, it might not always do what is best for humans.

DEEPFAKES

Deepfakes are pictures or videos made by AI. They blend sounds and images to create something that is not real. For example, AI may swap two people's faces. Or it may imitate someone's voice. Deepfakes can cause many problems. They can make it seem as if people did things they didn't actually do.

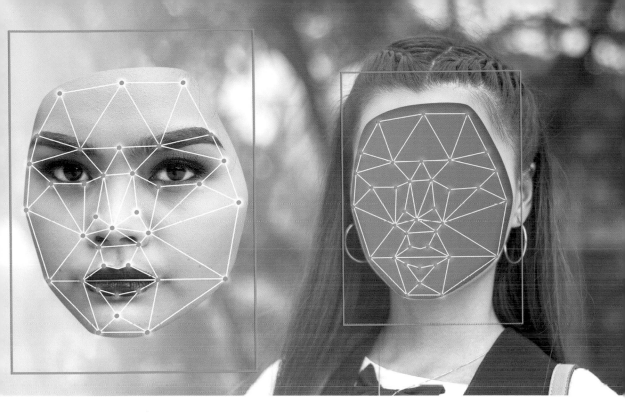

To make a deepfake, AI can copy one person's face and add it to a different image.

The spread of fake news on **social media** is one example. AI chooses what posts people see. Fake news stories often get lots of attention. So, AI spreads the stories, even though they are false. Many people worry that other choices made by AI could cause even greater harm.

CHAPTER 5

THE FUTURE OF AI

Today, AI already does many tasks that are difficult or time-consuming for people. As AI improves, it could do even more tasks. Robots could take over jobs that are simple or repetitive. People would be free to do more complex or interesting work. However, some people might have trouble finding jobs.

Robotic arms already do many jobs in factories. That way, human workers can do safer tasks.

One big concern is that AI can be biased against people because of their skin color or ethnicity.

AI could also help predict crimes and attacks. **Facial recognition** software could identify and track criminals. However, this process has risks. Innocent people could be blamed. People might also be unfairly spied on.

Governments are taking steps to protect people's privacy. Rules limit the data companies can collect. They require companies to ask users for permission. Researchers are finding safer ways to store people's information. They're also trying to prevent **hacks**. This work is important to using AI well in the future.

WILL AI TAKE OVER?

Some people fear that AI will become so smart that it will take over the world. Experts debate how likely that is to happen. AI already controls parts of many finance and medical systems. But most AI still needs huge amounts of data to do simple actions. So, AI cannot yet mimic some types of thinking.

FOCUS ON
ARTIFICIAL INTELLIGENCE

Write your answers on a separate piece of paper.

1. Write a paragraph describing the main ideas of Chapter 2.

2. Do you think the benefits of using AI outweigh the risks? Why or why not?

3. What is an algorithm?
   - **A.** a set of instructions for a computer
   - **B.** a picture or video created by AI
   - **C.** a person who uses social media

4. How does AI decide what content to show people on social media?
   - **A.** AI shows all users of social media the same content.
   - **B.** AI decides what to show people based on what content is most accurate.
   - **C.** AI decides what to show people based on what other users liked or shared.

Answer key on page 32.

GLOSSARY

biases
Unfair beliefs about a certain person or group of people.

context
The words or phrases that surround a specific part of a text and help people understand what it means.

data
Information collected to study or track something.

facial recognition
Using images of people's faces to figure out their identities.

fraud
The crime of tricking others in order to get money or information.

hacks
Times when people illegally gain access to information on computer systems.

social media
Forms of communication that allow people to connect on the internet.

software
Computer programs that perform certain functions.

TO LEARN MORE

BOOKS

Abell, Tracy. *Artificial Intelligence Ethics and Debates.* Lake Elmo, MN: Focus Readers, 2020.

Felix, Rebecca. *Artificial Intelligence: Can Computers Take Over?* Minneapolis: Abdo Publishing, 2019.

Leigh, Anna. *Cutting-Edge Artificial Intelligence.* Minneapolis: Lerner Publications, 2019.

NOTE TO EDUCATORS

Visit **www.focusreaders.com** to find lesson plans, activities, links, and other resources related to this title.

INDEX

Answer Key: 1. Answers will vary; **2.** Answers will vary; **3.** A; **4.** C